The Transparent Organization:

Unveiling the Secrets to Building an
Engaged and Self-Managing
~~Company~~ Community

Amanda Piotrowski Mulhearn

Based on a concept by John Bews

The Transparent Organization

Published by:
90-Minute Books
302 Martinique Drive
Winter Haven, FL 33884
www.90minutebooks.com

Published in the United States of America

ISBN-13: 978-0692506035
ISBN-10: 0692506039

For more information on 90-Minute Books including finding out how you can
publish your own lead generating book, visit www.90minutebook.com or call
(863) 318-0464

Special Thanks

Amanda Piotrowski Mulhearn would like to thank the following people for their help and support during the writing process.

John Bews, for the idea, inspiration, leadership, freedom, and opportunity that went into this – and every – project.

Rory Braine, for his cover art modeling skills, and Michele Whalen, for her cover art photography skills.

Bill Kendrick, for a lot of things…it doesn't matter how I label them, it's 'semantics.'

Bryan Cripe, Janien Dixon, Michelle Smith, Charise Triggiano, and Ryan Hague, for their continued reassurance that this would not be THE WORST!

Larry the Rashman for my first redlines.

The entire team at Davis Bews Design Group for giving me something to talk about, for their support, for participations in Transparent Organization surveys and interviews, and for being the face of the first generation of the T.O.

My husband Patrick Mulhearn, for proofreading, encouraging, and wine-pouring.

My parents Stanley and Valerie Piotrowski, and my sisters Ashley and Allison, for reading all of my 'work stuff' and actually caring…or at least faking it really, really well and for teaching me what NOT to do when smiling.

My new Mulhearn family for the laughs, the love, and the salt – I can't wait to take you in my spaceship.

Dan Sullivan, Shannon Waller, and the entire Strategic Coach team for teaching me about the 4 Cs and helping me find the confidence to complete this project.

You, for taking the time to read this far.

Here's What's Inside…

Start Me Up

(Foreword)

This book is designed to introduce you to the fundamental building blocks necessary to become a member of our Transparent Organization community. It is by no means all-inclusive. Reading it will not transform your company, your employees, or yourself. It won't give you all of the answers to all of your questions. It may not even compel you to read past the first chapter.

It is, however, designed to share with you an overview of a number of solutions we've put into place, tested, and perfected over the last 20+ years of operation. Our owner, John Bews (JB) – along with his business partner, Vice-President John Wagner – have spent the last couple of decades building a residential design and drafting firm in Oldsmar, Florida, which operates with fidelity under all of the tenets described in the subsequent chapters.

I can also say that this book is a tangible manifestation of pretty much everything it preaches, cover to cover. It was created under a totally self-managing (and engaged) model. JB wanted a book. I have a genuine interest in writing, and degrees in English and Business. So, JB paired his want with my (alleged) abilities, gave me some notes on cornerstones he wanted covered in the text, and set a deadline. I was then left on my own to put this future best-seller together. He won't have read it until it comes back from publishing, because he wanted freedom from its creation, while still having confidence it would be created. Now, whether it lives up to his expectations, I'll tell you in the sequel…or maybe somebody else will.

If you have a deft eye or took a few classes in Art Appreciation, you may notice that the graphics included appear to have been created on a miniscule budget. I promise, this is by design – they are all my original handiwork in Microsoft Paint, so our cost-investment in them was, obviously, about $0. You can choose your own adventure here as to why – either an ironic juxtaposition with our discussion of Unique Abilities® (Strategic Coach registered trademark) or an exercise in assessment of value creation (I determined the cost investment wouldn't produce even value to warrant its expense.) And regardless of whether my reader(s?) agree with all of my decisions, I was empowered to make them without consulting anyone else – and for better or for worse, I'll learn a lot from the entire process. And so will JB.

The Transparent Organization won't be for everyone, and if you're not sure if it's a good idea for your company, it probably isn't. Success in it requires a total commitment of the firm to all of its components. (A point of clarity here – we've learned, as we've grown, that not every employee will be able to successfully uphold or appreciate every aspect, all the time. It is important to ensure a balance of right-fit employees in your organization who can, collectively, uphold the individual pillars. We have learned the importance of achieving stability in balance and support in our infrastructure, and have come to find that it is just as important as having balanced support in the details of our residential floor plans.)

If any of the following four ideas in this list make you insurmountably uncomfortable, the T.O. probably isn't for you:

Zero Micro-Management: Entrust your team to make decisions on their own – even if, sometimes, they make the wrong ones. Learn from them.

Little 'Hierarchy': The Transparent Organization model functions best when the team members are on a level playing field – this includes you the entrepreneur, too. Obviously, there *are* fundamental separations of 'power' and 'authority,' but the more fluid and open to change the entire office is, the better.

Being Humble: We contend that everyone has a specialized skill set and can make exponentially valuable contributions in the right environment. The T.O. doesn't function in a room full of peacocks.

Embracing the Touchy-Feely: You don't have to take up writing sonnets or fill your office with a Precious Moments® menagerie, but bring a little appreciation, compassion, and humanity into your office – and encourage everyone on your team to do the same. Treat people like people.

If that list didn't scare you, then let's keep going!

Our business model is designed to empower an entire staff to be totally self-sufficient (and happy in their self-sufficiency) so that the owner can reap the benefits of his or her years of hard work by achieving freedom. Freedom *to* what? Freedom *from* what? The answers are abundant and endless, but fundamentally simple: whatever you, the entrepreneur, *want*. Whether it's to travel for a year, to pursue new bigger futures, or just to sit at home and catch up on all of the episodes of *Everybody Loves Raymond* you've missed over your own last decade or two of building a company, successful implementation of the Transparent Organization will allow committed business owners to move towards that freedom with confidence that their companies are in good, happy hands.

As you move through this book, you may find some of my rhetorical strategies to be…unconventional. We're kind of weird here, so I didn't want to hold any of that back. You may find yourself feeling excluded from a number of inside jokes or references. This book is about the people I work with, and this first iteration is, in part, a tribute and thank you to them. We'd have nothing to write about without them. As the front cover states, we haven't just built a company, we've built a *community*, and as we continue to propagate the Transparent Organization to our friends, colleagues, clients, and the world, we hope that our community continues to grow larger and larger – and that one day, you'll be a part of our inside jokes, too. And if you are interested in learning more about us and the way we do things, you can visit our blog at www.thetransparentorganization.com **www.davisbewsdesigngroup.com**.

You'll likely also notice some creative liberties I took with style[1] and tone. At times, it dabbles in self-deprecation, English-snobbery, sarcasm,

---

[1] For example, I use a lot of footnotes that may or may not be of any use to you along the way.

crassness, and ridiculousness[2]. Full transparency (though it'll probably be clear soon if it's not already): I've never written a book before. So I wrote this for myself as much as I did for you (my reader) or for JB. I'm sure I've made some mistakes, in content or in judgement, but my work under the Transparent Organization has led me to look forward to learning from them. If I didn't try this, once, I'd never have the courage to try it again. So, love it, hate it, forget you've ever even heard of it – but I encourage you to be as Transparent in your feedback with us as we've tried to be with you.

---

[2] Another example: several of the chapters conclude with a section that I've tactfully labeled *"I Call BS!"* These sections are designed to – hopefully – address and mitigate some of the doubts or yeah right! moments you might experience as you're reading through some of my more Utopian summaries.

Chapter One: I Need to Know
(A Case for Sharing Information With
ANYONE Who Will Listen)

People want to know stuff.

I probably just blew your mind, I know, but before you dismiss me as a total moron, I beseech you: be the Taylor to my Kanye and just let me finish, so that I may prove you wrong – or right.

Think about every little kid you've ever met. What is the most over-used word in a four-year old's vernacular?[3] Does this scenario look familiar?

"Donkeys are animals" – rational Adult who thinks he is just making a basic statement.

"Why?" – Four-Year-Old determined to ruin the rest of the 45-minute car ride.

"…because they're in the animal kingdom." – Adult, confident that his 4-year old companion will be satisfied with this taxonomic, scientific answer.

"Why?" – Four-Year-Old, who has not yet learned the 7 different kingdoms of living things and therefore has zero confidence in Adult's answer.

"…well, they are multicellular, which eliminates 'eubacteria' and 'archaebacteria' as possibilities…" – Adult, certain that this polysyllabic attempt to bore or frustrate the child will end this line of questioning.

---

[3] Not based on any actual data or research.

"Why?" – Four-Year-Old, who will not be stopped by words that may confuse or overwhelm him. He is determined to find the answer.

"It's really very complicated" – Adult, now growing frustrated for having to explain his answers. He's in charge. He knows what he's talking about. Why isn't this good enough? Adult has better things to do.

"Why?" – Four-Year-Old, desperate to get some truth and enlightenment. Adult initiated the conversation; Adult apparently has knowledge to support his opening statement. Why is adult being so withholding?

And on and on and on. You get the picture, you've been there before. You've probably even been that kid. Sure, sometimes the purpose is solely to be obnoxious and 'funny;' sometimes it's simply to fill conversational lulls. But mostly, it's because people have an innate desire to be informed. It's why we gossip; it's how Google became a verb; it's who we are.

That thirst for knowledge doesn't end in adolescence. Little things, big things, pivotal things, trivial things…we have a need to prove that we are right, or to have others prove to us that they are right.

How many times a week do you overhear (or participate in) below conversation?

"Was it Jeff Bridges or Jeff Daniels who starred in *The Big Lebowski?*" - Friend 1.

"I'm pretty sure it was Jeff Daniels. It was right before he did that movie about the grocery store dog…what was that movie called again? It had Dave Matthews starring as a mildly retarded pet shop worker." - Friend 2.

"No, that was *Because of Winn-Dixie*, which was Jeff Daniels. But Dave Matthews plays a mildly retarded man on an episode of *House*, not in that movie. I'm pretty sure it was Jeff Bridges in Lebowski." – Friend 1.

"You're both stupid. *The Big Lebowski* was in '98 with Bridges. *Winn-Dixie* (based on the 2001 Kate DiCamillo Newberry-medal winning novel of the same title, by the way) was in 2005, way after *Lebowski*, and was with Daniels. Matthews has played a semi-to-severely retarded man in seven different cinematic productions. Mark it an 8, dudes." – Know-It-All on the neighboring bar stool, courtesy of his next generation iPhone and lightning-fast ninja typing skills.

We all kind of hate that guy for chiming in with his answers, like he directed the damned movies himself. Mind your own business! Whatever happened to good ol' conversation? But also, we kind of love him, because lingering questions and unresolved curiosities drive us crazy. We want evidence. We want confidence. We want trust. If we didn't, the technology that enables guys like Know-It-All wouldn't be the bajillion dollar a month industry[4] that it is today. We all want to be the smartest guy (or girl – my apologies to my feminist audience for the abundance of male pronouns thus far) in the room…and if we can afford the fastest data plans, the title is at a fingertip's reach.

And it's not just trivia. People want to know what's in store. What's ahead? They want to avoid surprises. We check return addresses on envelopes before we peruse their contents. We look through peep holes before we answer our front doors. We check Caller ID before we commit to taking a phone call – and often will reject a number that we don't know or can't research quickly enough…we want to know who we're dealing with before we're forced to deal with them.

---

[4] Source: *Fortune 500* magazine

Knowledge offers at least one of two integral and irresistible benefits:

Point 1: Knowledge Fosters Engagement

You know that feeling you get when someone tries to make you look at 374 of their vacation photos to some place you'll never afford to visit, or their wedding you weren't invited to, or their child you didn't help sire? If you're ~~a big jerk~~ a normal person, like me, you probably try for a few minutes to garner or feign interest, but quickly glaze over and quit paying attention. Neurologists[5] across the globe posit that it is physically impossible for the synapses to bridge connections with images for which we have no foundation of knowledge or common familiarity.

Remember that high school or college class you took where you never had any idea what was going on? Or when your significant other comes home with 17 *hilarious* stories about what happened in the office today – can you believe that Charise in administration sent out ANOTHER cat picture? Most people in these situations totally zone out. It's very difficult to stay enthralled in an anecdote or lesson when you don't have the context for what's going on or who the key players are.

---

[5] No, I can't name any specifically – please accept this footnote as evidence supporting its own claim.

Charise, resident cat lady

As we saw in our example above, when Adult tried to dismiss Four-Year-Old's questions by burying them under confusing, jargony terms – this tactic doesn't work. The audience knows when this is being done to them. They're not stupid, even if they don't get all of your literary or scientific references. If you're not going to take the time to clue them in to the joke, then you don't look smart, you just look like a pretentious ass. And let's be honest, much like the cerebrally impaired Christian de Neuvillette[6] in *Cyrano de Bergerac*[7], you probably used your Google 'brain' for half of those gaudy allusions, anyway.

Instead of hoarding information, or being exclusive about when and with whom we will share it, we should publish it to anyone who's willing to hear what we know. If more people around us are interested in the same things we are, the more we'll be engaged with what they're talking about – and vice-versa. More importantly, however, the more collectively intelligent and dialed in our group is, the more quickly and efficiently we can all make progress – real, measurable progress. The smaller and fewer the gaps in understanding between all members in a team, the more moonshot the levels of accomplishment that team will realize.

The burden of closing knowledge gaps, though, usually falls unfairly on the audience. This may be because we assume our audience has context. It

---

[6] Christian de Neuvillette was a character in the 1897 play *Cyrano de Bergerac* who used the French version of Google to win the affections of his town's #1 searched-for woman.
[7] Or, as 1980s Americans know it, the Steve Martin blockbuster movie *Roxanne*.

may be intentional – we try to keep information on a 'needs-to-know' basis. It may simply because we, like Polonius, believe that brevity is the soul of wit. But whatever the reason, if the speakers or leaders are not providing enough backstory, or are being intentionally withholding or unclear, the audience is tasked with the responsibility to ask questions or to perform follow up research. Unfortunately, there are many reasons why people don't want to take these steps.

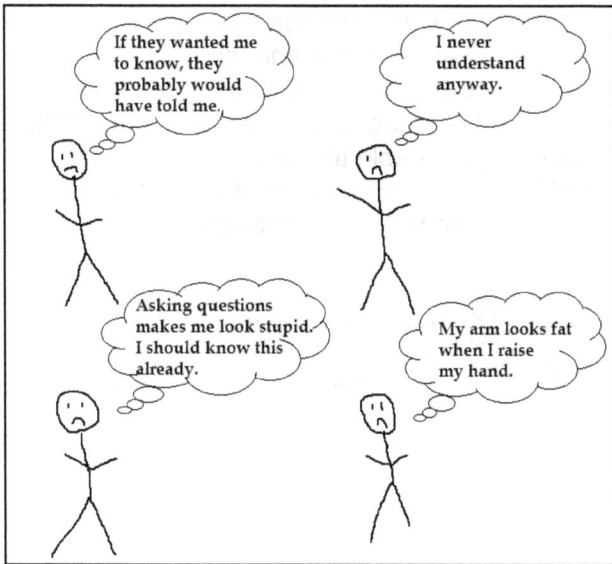

Point Two: Knowledge Yields Trust

Earlier, I alluded to the success of privacy-squashing innovations such as Caller ID. People feel safer and more inclined to engage when they know with whom they're dealing. Services like Angie's List prove that they will even pay a premium to know who the disreputable contacts are and to weed them out.

Even more importantly, when you offer a person knowledge and understanding, you are satisfying the Four-Year-Old that still resides somewhere inside his or her subconscious. Giving them the 'why' – as well as the whos and the hows and the whatnots, allows them to put a purpose to an action or decision. The more they understand something, the more they'll be able to support it and to take ownership of their own role within the initiative. Need proof? See the example below.

REAL-LIFE REENACTMENT, VERSION 1

REAL-LIFE REENACTMENT, VERSION 2

Now, which of those scenarios do you think yielded better results? In Version 1, the end result is that Little James did not trust Mr. Ryan, and he probably suffered severe poisoning and organ damage – or at least some serious regurgitation. In Version 2, however, Mr. Ryan provided context for Little James, as well as an indication that he is genuinely concerned for the youngster's welfare. Here, not only does Little James make a prudent decision based on information, he is appreciative of Mr. Ryan's pedagogy and has learned the dangers of imbibing toxic home chemicals! Also, how strange and unfortunate is it that two pairings of two people with the same exact names, placed in the same exact situations, could realize such different end results![8]

Even more dangerous than ingested bleach, however, can be the poison of secrecy. Sometimes, protected or privatized knowledge can create perceived tiers of hierarchy within a group. These hierarchal boundaries can inhibit the level of trust between members. The more tiers within an organization, whether they are intentional and distinct or accidental and ambiguous, the less freedom of communication that will occur between parties. Information becomes almost a currency,

---

[8] V1 Mr. Ryan is in prison for child negligence. No one comes to visit him, ever, and he lives solely on prune juice. V2 Mr. Ryan has a strong relationship with nephew Little James. Little James was so inspired by the life lesson that he conducted his OWN research, and was able to help Mr. Ryan expand his knowledge of healthy beverage options to a variety of fruit juices, all of which taste much better than prune.

and is traded with high frequency among an 'affluent' few and denied to the rest.

Instead, a regular stream of organization-wide updates, on pretty much every topic that does not compromise an individual's privacy, can work not only to keep everyone well-informed, but eliminates time lost due to hallucination and rumor-milling. There is no need for anyone to speculate as to what is going on, or why it is happening, and the natural predilection to formulate answers to unknowns will be removed. People won't waste time taking action in what they *think might* be the right direction – they'll be given all of the information to make decisions up front, and can act rationally and accordingly – and they'll appreciate the peace of mind, too.

Sharing Knowledge Eliminates Scarcity-Minded Hallucinations Like This Dramatic Real Life Re-Enactment:[9]

---

[9] I don't understand Clash of Clans.

With the right group of people, you may even find that they are so appreciative of and inspired by the information you're provided, they are able to connect some dots[10] on their own, and take the initiative to act on them. Often, they'll actually even spawn ideas or solutions you had never considered, rooted in their own Unique Abilities – a concept whose value we'll explore in-depth in a few chapters. (as Samuel L. Jackson would say, in the face of such anticipation, "hold on to your butts.")

There are myriad ways to realize the goal of transparency, and as you continue your journey through this page-turner, we'll help you connect the dots[11] as to how it can work in your own organization.

---

[10] Like drinking games? Have a sip of your favorite beer, wine, or cocktail every time we say 'connect the dots.' It'll make the book way more enjoyable, very quickly. Not a fan of drinks? Pop a vitamin – I don't know if vitamins have any effect on amusement, but you'll definitely be able to skip your apple for the day.

[11] Seriously, hit up your fridge or Vitamin cabinet

Chapter Two: Easy Like Sunday Morning (Systemization of *Everything*)

One of the most fundamental components of the Transparent Organization is the systematizing and simplifying of all of our processes. We document everything and use uniform instructions for how to do everything. I mean, everything. We also have procedures and formulas in place for nearly every back-office task we complete. It might sound like a lot of work to build, but we consistently build them as we develop new needs, so it really ends up being a minimal time investment on the front-end that saves us lots of time and agony down the line.

When I first started work at DBDG, I was given about a bajillion documents (in both electronic and paper format) called Unique Methods® (a Strategic Coach product strikes again) which detailed how to do anything that I would need to know to complete my job. I mean anything. How to update and save information in Excel, how to process new work when it came into the office, how to create invoices in our project management software, et cetera. Most of the times, the idea of creating and following these documents made plenty of obvious sense: we all had consolidated instructional manuals, like any other job.

However, the requests for UMs became, in my opinion, ridiculous. I remember answering one of my 17 million daily phone calls from Bill, asking me to prepare three different UMs on how to send three different types of emails to three different sets of recipients. It was (at the time) the stupidest thing I'd ever heard. Everyone knows how to send an email! I hung up the phone (which Bill probably just called again 10 seconds later – he's the fastest dial in the West Tampa) and started grumbling about how meticulous and nit-picky he was being.

Actual[12] Sample UMs from Our Office

---

[12] Nope. But Charise will probably post the third one if she ever gets around to reading this.

How to Open the Front Door
(From Outside)

1. Determine if the door is locked by twisting the handle in a clockwise motion.

2. If the door opens, walk inside. If it does not, proceed to Step 3.

3. Find the gold key on your key ring that articulates with the lock.

4. Turn the key to the right.

5. Open the door.

6. Remove your key.

7. See Step 2.

How to Turn on Your Computer
(Laptop Version)

1. Lift the screen until it is at a 90 degree angle if it is not already so.

2. Find the power button and depress it for about 2 seconds.

3. Wait patiently as the computer loads up.

4. Select your user profile from the login screen.

5. Enter your password. Be sure to spell it correctly.

How to PROPERLY Wash Your Hands

1. Run the sink water to a lukewarm temperature.

2. Apply a quarter-sized amount of soap to your hands.

3. Work the soap into a later and work back and forth under the sink for 20 - 30 seconds.

4. Turn off the water.

5. Dry your hand with a paper towel, thoroughly.

6. Do NOT forget to apply lotion immediately after.

I was right – sort of. We are extremely, compulsively detailed. We record the 'hows' of everything we do, which I came to accept, but did not see the value in. What was missing for me was the 'whys' of doing so – which came shortly after I left my position working with Bill and had to train someone else to be my lucky replacement (you're welcome, Pretty Thickness). It became obvious to me how useful all of the UMs I had made could be to someone starting a new job from scratch – and how all of the UMs I had de-prioritized making would be helpful, if they existed. The whole purpose of the copious documentation is to achieve future efficiency – anybody can come in, and, with the correct series of UMs, replicate anybody else's job. We have found that there is zero value in hoarding knowledge – instead, documenting all of our knowledge allows us to keep moving in the event of emergency, and facilitates quick shifting of responsibilities as we constantly evolve in our own roles.

Cindy, one of our top Process-Oriented performers, plugging away at some processy process. Look how happy she is!

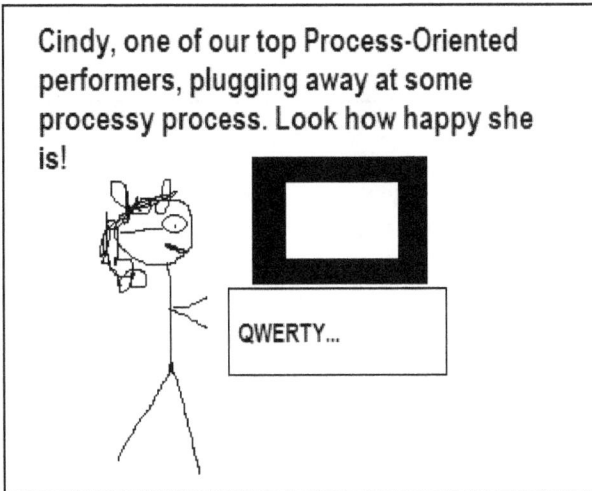

QWERTY...

Our simplification of processes doesn't end with instructions, though. There is rhyme and reason to nearly everything we do. When we receive new projects from our clients, for example, they are all given a project number. Those numbers are all 'codes' that identify which client the project belongs to and the year in which it is started. They are controlled by a preexisting database, and automatically assigned to new work and new clients as needed. The project numbers are used to help us organize files (both electronic and physical); to track job cost average of each individual job we take in; and to uniquely identify each individual plan. An exciting sample is below. [13]

> **ACTUAL SAMPLE (For Real This Time): The DBDG Project Log** – This document organizes project numbers and dictates what the next item should be. There is a section for New Product, a section for Lot Specifics, and a section for Occasional Custom work. Adherence to this list allows for simplified reporting, organization, and data analysis.

---

[13] You'll note that we marked some information out. Even *we* draw the line at being transparent (externally) about our client information...but at least we're transparent about wanting our privacy!

		DBDG PROJECTS 2014			

		***PLEASE ENTER ALL INFORMATION IN CAPS FOR CONSISTENCY			
FS NO.	CLIENT	PROJECT DESCRIPTION	SCOPE OF SERVICES	PM	Date Assigned
24-000					
24-001	▬	LOT SPECIFICS	LOT SPECIFIC	DK	1/2/2013
24-002	▬	LOT SPECIFICS	LOT SPECIFIC	DK	1/2/2013
24-003	◢	LOT SPECIFICS - MISC COMMUNITIES	LOT SPECIFIC	BK	1/2/2013
24-004	▬	LOT SPECIFICS	LOT SPECIFIC	JC	1/2/2013
24-005	▬	CAD LOT SPECIFICS	LOT SPECIFIC	JD	1/2/2013
24-006					
24-007					
24-008	▬	LOT SPECIFICS - ▬	LOT SPECIFIC	BK	1/2/2013
24-009			LOT SPECIFIC		
24-010	▬	LOT SPECIFICS - ▬	LOT SPECIFIC	BK	1/2/2013
24-011	▬	▬ S COUNTRY CLUB	TOWNHOME	BK	1/14/2014
24-012	▬	▬ - LOT SPECIFICS	LOT SPECIFIC	BK	1/28/2014
24-013	▬	HAYES PARK COTTAGES	LOT SPECIFIC	BP	2/12/2014
24-014	▬	MARION COTTAGE	LOT SPECIFIC	BP	2/12/2014
24-015	▬	▬	DDs / CDs	BK	
24-016	▬	LOT SPECIFICS	LOT SPECIFIC	BP	4/2/2014
24-017	▬	LOT SPECIFICS	LOT SPECIFIC	JD	1/1/2014
24-018	▬	LOT SPECIFICS - ▬	LOT SPECIFIC	BK	5/21/2014
24-019	▬	LOT SPECIFICS	LOT SPECIFIC	JD	1/1/2014
24-020	▬	▬ LOTS	LOT SPECIFIC	BK	3/8/2014

Another behind-the-scenes treat for you: all of our project managers maintain Client Status Reports (CSRs) for each of their clients. These reports allow us to systematically track the (you guessed it) status of all projects and floor plans we maintain, and ALSO help us establish transparency with our clients as to the progress we're making on our work for them. The reports are updated no less than weekly (sometimes, multiple times daily, depending on the volume of their work). They are shared internally all day, every day, and then are sent to the clients at week-end.

Footage From a Real Client Status Report!

We have also developed a series of mostly-
automated metrics to let us know how well we are
performing in pursuit of our financial goals (or
where we need to improve). With only minimal
effort on the parts of our reporting team, we are
able to get current information in a matter of
minutes, for many of our important statistics. As
previously mentioned, we track job cost averages –
on an individual, client, and company-wide basis, to
ensure that we are beating our minimum target
dollar-per-hour earning. The drill downs to client
and job-specific allows us to identify improvement
opportunities and areas of inefficiency.
Additionally, we assign and track individual
employee statistics – items such as utilization rates
(number of billable hours worked by employees)
and Quality Assurance scores (all plans created by
our production department are put through a strict
review process to ensure adherence with our
standards of excellence). And of course, there are
statistics on how we are performing company-wide.
How much have we invoiced in proportion to our
monthly and annual goals? How do our actual
three-month projections compare to our goal

forecast? What is the breakdown of our accounts receivable, and what is being done to minimize its total balance?

All of the information above – and many, many other statistics, too – is made public to the entire staff. At any time, Sergio can review Bradley's QA average or see how close to or far from his u-rate goal he's performing. Also noteworthy, in this example, Sergio is (presently) Bradley's fledgling direct employee. It's not common that performance metrics are so accessible, especially looking 'up' the hierarchy. Anybody can see statistics on anyone else in the company, if they want to.

Now, this may seem invasive, or punitive or even embarrassing to someone who is struggling, or new, or who has made some mistakes. And it may be, at times, if you're at the low end of the spectrum, regardless of the reason. But we've found that is way more useful and incentivizing the way that we do it. These published numbers actually drive both self-management and engagement on our team. Since everyone knows how everyone else is doing (and everyone KNOWS that everyone else knows, and so on), there is more incentive to produce – no one wants to be the community pariah for extended periods of slack and sub-par performance. The numbers actually work to fuel healthy levels of competition between employees, as seen below:

The Pam-Pilar QA Feud of 2014[14]

---

[14] Both Pam and Pilar are much prettier than this. Also, we are actually provided with very comfortable and accommodating furniture, and keyboards with all 26 letters and a bunch of numbers and special characters, too, but I already spent like 5 hours just to draw this set-up, so...

The public numbers help keep us all accountable not only for ourselves, but each other. If we recognize patterns in people that show they could benefit from some assistance, we go find ways to remedy it. Likewise, if we find patterns of excellence, we start looking to see what is working there, and how to duplicate and spread it to improve the whole team. And we're able to do this very efficiently, because 1) we don't have to wait for anyone to tell us there is a problem/opportunity – enough of us care enough to find it on our own; and 2) we don't have to sit through days and weeks of bureaucratic red tape and permission slips. If we see something worth talking about or fixing, we just go do it. Transparency of information breeds transparency of conversation.

We try to make all of the information as understandable as possible. We actually go over the highlights together during our weekly Team Focus Meeting, the subject of a later chapter. We report the most crucial figures in just 5 simple dials, which track our progress toward annual goals around billable hours, invoiced projects, job cost average, projections, and accounts receivable. Many other statistics and figures are reviewed by smaller groups or individuals, but again, they are all available to anyone who wants to see them.

Chapter Three: Brass in Pocket
(A Collective Effort to Capitalize on Our Individual Strengths)

I'm a terrible interviewee. I'll never understand how I got this job at DBDG, but I will be eternally grateful for it.

In real life, I'm actually pretty gregarious. I love to be surrounded by people. I am animated when storytelling and dialed-in when story-listening. I rarely shy away from the limelight and pride myself on being authentic and open about who I am. But in interview mode, I completely shut down. I become so focused on whether my mascara is clumping - or my voice is cracking - or whether my verbiage in Q-and-A is perceived as erudite or sesquipedalian - that I completely disconnect from the conversation altogether. I go through all of the motions, but am completely devoid of any panache or charm[15].

Truth be told, I only really remember one question from the entire interview process; partly because of the uniqueness of the question itself and partly because of my answer (although that answer has come to be a huge part of what I love about my job, I'm sure it only stuck out in memory because of its fantastic balance between inarticulateness and potential to be misconstrued as 7th-grade-style sexual harassment). My response, though I had no way of knowing at that time, was to become the

---

[15] In the interest of full transparency, I should probably confess that I don't ever have charm or panache.

cornerstone of what I love most about the Transparent Organization and DBDG.

As I sat across a long wooden table from Bryan, trying not to focus on the charmingly incongruous expensive-looking conference room leather chairs with the frat-party reminiscent red Solo cup in which I had been served water, he asked me the best interview question I've ever heard. "In three years, what has to have happened for you to be happy with your progress?"

It really isn't that far off a question from its bastardized cousin "What is your five-year plan?" but there was something about its phrasing that just really landed with me. It seemed to lend itself more to my wants and my expectations. Three years seemed more realistic and tangible than five years. And somehow, it didn't immediately open the door to focus on dollars and titles, as the standard version does. I found my answer quickly – a little too quickly, maybe, given my poor diction – but it was the most honest and 'me' moment of the interview.

"I want a *thing*," I responded. "I want a *thing*, and I want everyone to know that I have a *thing*, and I want everyone to come to me when they want *that thing.* And the longer I work here, I want to make that *thing* better and better, and I want a reputation of being trusted for being the one who is good with that *thing.*"

Luckily, middle school me didn't listen to that answer until well after the interview was over. I didn't know at the time that there was a middle school Bryan (I now know there is ONLY a middle school Bryan, who just masquerades as an adult on Halloween and St. Patrick's Day), but he too kept his composure. In fact, he acted like this was a GOOD answer, and one that pleased him.

And that was the first time I heard the phrase "Unique Ability®."

Now, let me first disclose that this phrase is not a DBDG, John Bews, or Transparent Organization brainchild. It is actually a concept packaged and promoted by Dan Sullivan, of Strategic Coach. We incorporate many practices and philosophies created by Dan, so we'll be giving our propers to Coach a few times throughout this text.

Bryan went on to explain to me that we actually had a term for exactly what I had described – Unique Ability® (UA). It was relatively new in implementation across the office at the time – and even today, it is not ubiquitously in effect – but every time someone gets to work in his or her UA, they shine. The idea is so simplistic and obvious, but it requires self-awareness (on the parts of the individuals within the firm AND of the firm as a whole) and team-awareness. Basically, EVERYONE is encouraged to identify his or her truly special "thing" and to do that thing as often as possible.

I was sold. I couldn't wait to find my *thing* and show it to everyone and use it all the time. Trouble was, I had no idea what my UA would be. And when I started asking around, a lot of my colleagues didn't know theirs, either. I thought maybe it was just more corporate jargon and false hope cultivation, and tabled my UA quest to focus on the job I'd been hired to do.

Over time, however, I found myself inundated with projects and opportunities. I had a steady queue that would have, and should have, been easy to manage without missing deadlines. But I subconsciously (well, maybe a little consciously) became guilty of putting off tasks that bored me, or that I knew I could do quickly and easily – Excel updates, invoicing. I also put off tasks that frustrated or annoyed me (FILING!)[16], and moved the work that I found myself most interested in to the top of the pile. I found myself drawn to client communication – I was happier talking with clients

---

[16] We briefly employed someone who used the most beautiful filing system we've ever seen. He could practically make papers line up and obey his hand the way Miss Potts controlled dishes in *Beauty and the Beast* (or like Chris Pratt controlled raptors in *Jurassic World* – feel free to choose your own analogy). There really is a UA match for everything, somewhere out there.

about why they hadn't paid bills than I was generating those bills. Someone passed off to me some applications that required some writing, and I was totally thrilled! People started asking me to proofread documents, letters, emails – I was always so honored to get to do that work that I would delay some of the big parts of my job until they HAD to get done (this is a danger of picking up too much UA work too quickly – always make sure the work already in demand is covered somewhere).

When Keeping it Really UA Goes Wrong

In most jobs, that practice would probably get a girl (or a boy; we don't want to offend any masculinists, either) in a good bit of trouble after a while. You can't pick-and-choose the parts of your job you want to do; you do what you're hired to do, and that's it. But here, I actually found myself rewarded for it! I kept being given similar assignments to the ones I liked. People invited me to be part of projects, meetings, and proposals. Bill, my then-supervisor, would ask me to draft, what seemed to me to be, some pretty important conceptual documents for him because he was focused on designing or drafting (semantics, BK) in AutoCAD and I was a better "wordsmith." I LOVED the conceptual documents and was thrilled to take them off his English-muffin-and-sausage-stained proverbial plate.

It turned out, I was gradually growing into my *thing*. I've actually been lucky enough to find that I have a couple of *things*, but I believe that they're all derivative of my primary UA: words. I like learning them, teaching them, spelling them, using them, writing them, saying them, inverting them, analyzing them. For reasons that I can't put into words (the irony!), I've always found them indefatigably fascinating, and anytime I can find a new way to use them, I can't wait. And lucky for me, at DBDG, there is no one else who likes them quite as much as I do – or, at least, not as ostentatiously. I was able to take on more and more work like this because I was good at it, and a lot of my colleagues were less good (or less confident) at it.

Turns out, John Bews (and Dan Sullivan, and even Bill) are just a bunch of sneaky, wily, no-good tricksters! By finding out what I liked to do and do could well, they were able to:

Get higher-quality results on projects which matched my UA.

Free up people who were not good at word-oriented tasks so they could focus on their own…wait for it…UA skills.

Make me genuinely excited about and engaged in my work – so much so that I would just cry, like a Billy Idol heroine, for more, more, more.

What was even more shocking about it is that they were COMPLETELY TRANSPARENT from Day One about this devilishly genius plan. Bryan basically told me during the interview that it was their intention to prey on people's UAs, to pander to their professional addictions and exploit them, and I ate it right up. I emailed him for weeks to ensure I had the job – revealing my communication passion and UA before I even had an offer.

Obviously I wanted to pack all my things and leave immediately, but I had so many exciting emails, idea proposals, letters, forms, and other items waiting for me to create and/or proofread that I couldn't tear myself away. So I've been a slave to a job I love ever since. I continue to find new ways to create value for the company using my UA. And just when I think I've run out of ways to be useful, Ryan calls me to ask me how to spell "succinctly" or Bill asks me to remind him whether it's "accept" or "except," because he wasn't listening the first time[17]. And as long as it is outside of Bill's UA to pay attention to words, I'll have room to create value and work in a space (physical and positional) that keeps me truly happy and fascinated.

I'm not the only one who feels this way, either. Shawn and Scott, our primary designers, are deeply passionate

---

[17] He probably didn't listen the second time, either.

about their work and rabidly chase every opportunity to show off their abilities. During a recent IDP (detailed in an upcoming chapter), Scott even wrote "designing for DBDG is the future to my 40 years past in this business - it consists of everything I have ever wanted in my professional life."[18] Larry, our Quality Assurance guru, spends most of his time finding mistakes on people's plans and educating them on how not to make them again. Thankfully, if you're going to have someone spend all day showing you every single thing you do wrong, Larry's also got the UA to do so without making you want to punch him in the face.[19]

I'm Pretty Sure This Is How Redlines With Larry Typically Go...

---

[18] This is probably the only totally accurate quote in the entire text. BAM! Transparency strikes again.
[19] Even though I don't work in CAD, and therefore never produce floorplans, I too know this first-hand. Larry's QA gift transcends all media, written and spoken.

I Call B.S.!

Can you really hire and match up so perfectly that everyone gets to love every minute of every day of their jobs?

No, of course not. First of all, many of us do have more than one skill at which we excel and more than one interest we wish to indulge. In addition to having a full-sized vocabulary, I make excellent chicken parmesan and do really good impressions of pretty much everyone. I doubt I will ever need to use either of these superpowers in the workplace. Also, I have to do lots of things that I absolutely hate. I still have to file. I hate filling out my timesheet. One of my current projects involves developing a website to sell our custom-made plans all over the country, and I am ridiculously incompetent in my current role as a conduit between our CAD team (who are so brilliant at their work) and our potential customers. It's frustrating, and I feel completely incompetent, asking way too many questions that almost EVERYONE else in this company can answer even more easily than if they were asked for their social security numbers (although we do have one guy who doesn't even have to speak it – he tattooed his social onto his arm, so he may be excluded from this group.) However, the amount of time I DO get to devote to my UA more than offsets the frustrating parts of my job, and reinvigorate me with confidence and enthusiasm to power through the humdrum or intimidating.

In the continued interest of transparency, we did run into a problem of overstating our ability to let everyone work in their UAs all of the time – especially since we employ so many people of so many diverse talents. We do our best to highlight, celebrate, and utilize everyone's talents whenever possible.

That withstanding, we are fortunate work in an industry that really only attracts UA talent in the first place. Most of our drafters and designers are inherently great at drawing, designing, making things work, problem-solving, visualization, puzzles…pretty much everything I'm bad at. So, while many of our employees may not get a lot of opportunity to showcase ALL of their unique abilities all of the time, (Heath is a machine on the dance floor and Cari has a real talent for turning anything into a dirty joke), they still get to spend upwards of 80% of their time working at something they're truly good at.

Chapter Four: Where Are You Going? (Individual Development Plans)

The Transparent Organization model does not allow room for traditional employee evaluation meetings, as are standard practice in many corporate operating structures. We want our team members to grow, improve, and develop, of course – but since they are empowered to be self-managing, we have found that we see the most engagement in and progress from these sessions when the employees are in total control of them. Rather than a quarterly review, therefore, our employees prepare quarterly Individual Development Plans (IDPs).

REAL-LIFE SNAPSHOT OF A HAPPY EMPLOYEE DURING IDP SEASON!!!

IDP

REAL-LIFE RAINBOW

The exact composition of the IDP is constantly evolving as we learn more about what does and does not work for the majority of our team (the T.O. has proven that they have zero problem telling us), or as we find gaps in the program and solutions to them. But the purpose is consistent: the IDP is a platform for employees to tell us where THEY want to go and what THEY want to do. There are tools and forms in place to help set short and long-term goals, and milestones to accomplishing those goals. Also included are various 'rest stops' on the proverbial road to their personal goals to think more company-wide: questions centered on appreciation of others, core values, and personal contributions to team-wide metrics.

We have found that this system helps team members feel much more connected to and in control of their futures at DBDG. We've allowed people to work themselves into – and out of – positions or responsibilities in constant pursuit of maximizing time spent in UA, and minimizing time spent in wrong-fit roles and areas of accountability. We have a few success stories of talented individuals who worked themselves into promotions as Project Managers, only to find that they hated doing a large portion of the necessary work that went along with the jobs – not out of laziness or ineptitude, just the fact that they were so much stronger in other vital performance areas. Those people were able, through IDP goal setting and solution chasing, to re-work themselves into lateral moves that freed them up from the agonizing responsibilities their 'Management' roles required and instead made them exponentially more valuable to the company by working in capacities in which they happily excel.

Obviously, the fact that somebody writes something down on a piece of IDP paper does not make it law, truth, or even feasible. No matter how Kenny tells us that he wants to spend most of his on-the-clock time growing our anime mural department, we're probably not going to support him in his goal. But, he gets an hour a quarter to try and convince his supervisor that this is actually an opportunity for value creation – and that's where the game can totally change.

IDPs are individual employees' chances to show us their big-picture ideas, and to demonstrate why they are paths that are worth our pursuit. If they can outline clear steps to accomplish goals, plans for achieving them without compromising existing obligations and responsibilities, and byproducts (financial or other) of their realization, the odds are in their favor that we will green light their ideas. If an idea is underdeveloped, impractical, or ill-timed, it is never killed – it can be reengineered and reincarnated in another IDP. Often the tenacity in reoccurring ideas highlights their importance to the individuals and will incite deeper conversations about the goals and better clarity as to what is necessary for it to become a reality.

The IDP meetings can be equally effective at resolving smaller-picture goals that still have the potential to improve working conditions, equipment, or efficiency. They're a great platform for identifying productivity obstacles and solutions. Sometimes, budgetary, time, and capital restrictions may impede the ability to handle them right away, but by resurrecting them during quarterly sessions with supervisors, employees can be sure to keep them on the radar for when they are more feasible.

Based on a true story!!!!!

Of course, we try to make sure that no individual's IDP goals or wants come at the expense of another person. In an office of dozens of employees, it can be difficult for any supervisor to have tabs on the entire office's ambitions or needs. So, as a safety net, all IDP paperwork comes to a team of strategic planners (presently, me and that Bryan guy from the UA chapter[20]) to connect dots between goals, holes, and roles. We look for potentially missed opportunities, overlooked dangers, possible matches between UAs and needs across teams, and items that may need more clarification. We also look for teams of people interested in pursuing similar value-creation ideas and encourage them to share their ideas and work together to test or prove their validity. Sometimes, we are able to complete and close files on needs immediately after our joint

---

[20] Until this book gets me fired.

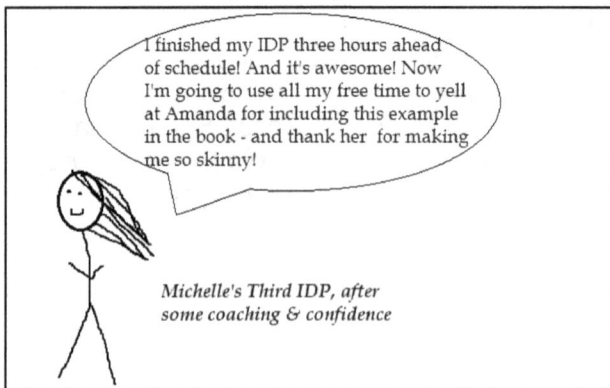

review, simply by what we've found in our reading. We then funnel our findings, questions, suggestions, and actionable items to any interested parties – then scramble to begin our own IDPs, which are intentionally staggered a few weeks behind the rest of the team.

We want all of the members of our office to be active contributors to our internal community, and we believe that the IDPs are one of the best ways to encourage activity. *Asking* employees open-ended questions about their goals and wants facilitates much more positive conversation and brainstorming about the future of the individuals and their potential to benefit the company than closed-ended, limited-perspective commands. The more people on our team who are constantly striving for growth and excellence, the more abundant the atmosphere we are all working in, and the faster our company can grow – while keeping its our team members fascinated and motivated in their jobs.

I Call BS!

Is everyone so excited about the IDP process?

No. For some employees, it is confusing. For some, it is a point of stress. For some, it is just a paperwork interruption in the workweek. A lot of employees drift in and out of engagement in the process, depending on a variety of factors, including personal sources of stress or distraction or uncertainty of the next logical career step. A handful of our employees are already working upwards of 90% in their ideal positions, and therefore see little need to strive for growth.

To make the process more valuable to these employees, we encourage them to focus on and plan for goals that are personal, instead of just professional, in nature. We understand that mothers (or fathers)-to-be, newly engaged, bereaved, or soon-to-be retiring employees might be more comfortable simply maintaining their work situations. We also recognize that not everyone WANTS to constantly change their roles and responsibilities – some people are happy to simply learn and master a craft. We now offer several different options to satisfy IDP requirements. For those who, for any reason, aren't ready to commit to any large-scale changes or goals, we have options which are a quick opportunity to focus on our culture, to scantly outline some future ambitions, and call it a wrap.

As we continue to grow in employee count, we've come to realize that it is actually extremely beneficial that not every individual is focused on achieving exponential individual growth every quarter. We want people who are committed to maintaining the foundation of our business – our clients are still our number one focus, and without their business we wouldn't have the revenue to fund bigger-future ideas and goals.

I think the lovely Rachel Green, from NBC's *Friends*, can sum up what I'm talking about better than I ever could. Take a minute to watch this clip from Season 6, Episode 13: "The One With Rachel's Sister," during which she tries to caution her spoiled sister Jill against the perils of making too many life changes at one time:

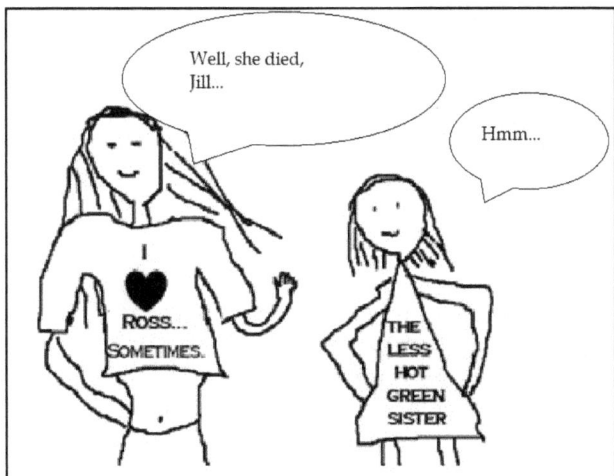

As Rachel astutely taught us, through this allegory about an over-ambitious woman who is in no way made up, if you try to do too many things at once, you'll likely end up making minimal progress – if not actually retrogressing in some areas.

Therefore, we have grown to embrace the reality that not every employee will pursue big goals at every IDP – in fact, some employees will not pursue big goals at ANY IDP. But they all have the freedom to, and they will all serve their own valuable purposes in sustaining the core of the company.

Chapter Five: I Guess You Had to Be There (The Team Focus Meeting)

In the interest of total transparency, this chapter is my greatest disappointment.[21]

I say this because the amount of time I've spent writing, erasing, and re-writing it feels as long as listening to a live version of the Allman Brothers' *Whipping Post* while stuck in rush-hour traffic. And while I love me some time with Duane, Gregg, and company, a large *je ne sais quoi* is forfeited if you're not in that live, energizing environment – where it feels like a concert and sounds like a concert (and usually smells likes a concert, too). I guess what I mean is that every time I conclude another version of this chapter, it feels like one of those jokes that ends with "I guess you had to be there."[22]

The focus of this section is our Team Focus Meeting, which occurs EVERY week, on Thursdays, from 9:30 until 10:15, without exception.[23] For me, and I hope for most of the staff, the meeting is the highlight of the week. It's a break from all the crushing it and goal-smashing that we do during the rest of our 40+ workweeks,

---

[21] Like, on par with the series finales of *Seinfeld* or *Dexter*, or U2's unforgivable *Put on Your Boots*.

[22] I used to think this phrase was a cop-out for people who are terrible storytellers. My apologies to all of the 'had-to-be-there-ers' I've scorned over the years.

[23] Exceptions: Thanksgiving Day and Christmas week.

and it's the only time that we all get to spend together. Employees are expected to attend this meeting every week with full fidelity, though absences are occasionally pardoned for pressing client deadlines, client meetings, airborne communicable disease, and Dave Matthews Band concert/Lightning game/Rays game recovery sessions.[24]

The meeting is the total culmination of all things transparent. Here, not only does the company take a moment to show all of its cards – financial standings, client leads, goals progress, any new developments or strategic directions – but also, each and every member of our team is offered a platform for total transparency of self. It is essential to helping us build and maintain the community feel we have within our own organization. During the week, we're semi-compartmentalized into teams and roles, and often have little time to really get to talk to our colleagues in other rooms or on other floors. But the TFM allows us to pause and communicate with one another. We learn a lot about each other in a very short allowance of time. Some of it might sound a little peace-pipe or hippie like…and maybe it is, but it really helps us adhere to some of our core values and protect our culture. Again, you'd probably have to be there to really get it.

---

[24] Just kidding. Client meetings are no excuse to miss a TFM.

A Typical Team Focus Meeting[25]

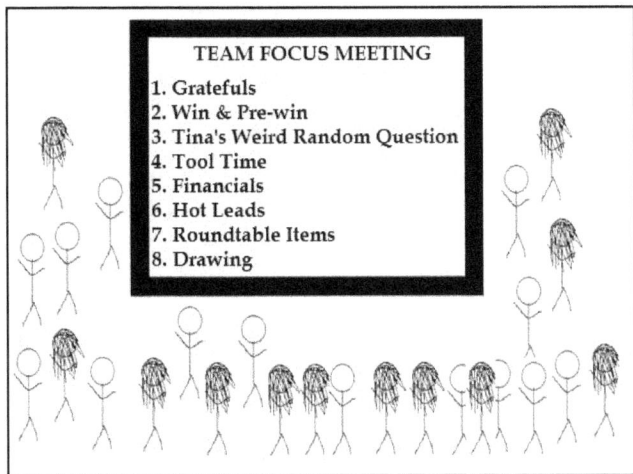

We begin with a sharing of our 'gratefuls.' Every week, a team member is selected at random to begin the dialogue, and simply lists off all the people, belongings, or events for which he or she is thankful. There is no 'formula': you can list one item or one hundred, so it never needs to be forced to hit some ideal (if we wanted the minimum to be 15 pieces of flair, we'd make the minimum 15 pieces of flair.) And there are certainly predictable staples: Janien is always thankful for her husband Bill and her daughter Kylee; Charise is always thankful for her cat Malcolm; Kendra is always thankful for her truck; Rory is always thankful for GAINS; Matt N. is always thankful for some low-budget brand of beer and the fact he showed up to work in spite of it. But there are also always fun or

---

[25] We actually all get to sit down. But again, chairs are difficult to draw. Also, not pictured: Scott. That pony tail can't be duplicated.

touching surprises. It's an opportunity to publicly express gratitude towards others in the office who have really stepped up during the last week; it's a chance to share something really personal; it's a chance to argue about sports teams' victories and losses. It was during the gratefuls sessions, over the last couple of years, that I learned that Matt H. is Canadian and that Eric likes to service his wife *and* her car (slips of the tongue rarely go unacknowledged in the TFM.) These 5 second stories are all some of my favorite memories of working at Davis Bews Design Group – but again, I guess you had to be there.

Once all thirty-something of us have listed our gratefuls, we move on to the 'wins' segment of the meeting. Here, we each humblebrag about our biggest accomplishments over the past week, then commit to the biggest accomplishments we plan to achieve over the next week. Sometimes, our achievements are simple and personal: three-day beach weekends, a good time at a concert, obtaining all of another colony's lions in Clash of Clans[26], or a drunken victory in another chapter of a Golden Tee rivalry at Winghouse. Other times, however, we have milestones to share out that we're really proud of: completion of large-scale projects, a gesture of appreciation or satisfaction from a client, the birth of a baby (or Canadian grandbaby), or the publication of a long-overdue and over-thought book. It's an opportunity for us to learn what our team members are dealing with,

---

[26] I still have no idea what people do when they play Clash of Clans, but I imagine this is how Andy from *Parks and Recreation* would handle it.

what they're excited about, and where we can offer them support.

Recently, we added a 'Question of the Week' to the rotation. This one is mainly for fun – and it's here, especially, that an HR department would shut down our entire operation. Sometimes it gets a little dirty, sometimes it gets a little curse-y, and sometimes it just gets plain weird. But it allows us all to really let our guards down, for even just a few minutes, and show the rest of our working community a little bit more of who we are and where our minds can go when they're free to think and express themselves without restriction. Work-related or not, you've got to appreciate the power of unbridled creativity.

The meeting usually takes a more work-focused turn for the second half of the meeting, as we move into the 'Tool of the Week.' This can be a PowerPoint, a video, an article, a game, or any other vehicle of pedagogy, but it is designed to somehow strengthen our team. We've done segments that are simply designed to encourage big-picture thinking; segments that are geared towards strengthening internal relationships; segments that reveal new strategic directions; segments that address new marketing ideas. The point is, though, that we spend a few minutes to collectively share an idea. It may not land with everyone, every time, but we hope we are able to help at least one person connect a dot that will lead to better results in some capacity.

The most important part, at least from a purely professional perspective, is the next segment, during which we publish our financial standings. We have predetermined weekly, monthly, quarterly, and annual goals, and we review our progress towards those goals every week during the financials discussion. First, we review where we were last week, to hold ourselves accountable for the progress we committed to making during our last meeting. Rarely do we fall short of our promised projections, but if we do, we're there to address the *why* and to redirect the team so that we can catch up. Most of the time, we get to celebrate the fact that we made more progress than anticipated, and thank the team for their contributions to that progress. We then evaluate the supporting metrics we've put in place to ensure we're on track to realizing our goals. We want everyone to know exactly how we're doing and why. This knowledge empowers every individual to understand what needs to be done and why, and gives them control to do whatever it takes to realize our goals.

We follow our financials discussion with a Hot Leads review, where we discuss all of the new and existing leads we've expected to turn into real jobs. If a lead is converted to a real job, we celebrate it. If a lead turns cold or is lost, we explain why, and, if it was preventable, try to learn from it. When the lead is brand new, we discuss where it came from and what we're doing to pursue it and keep it hot. The entire team can see what we're doing (or, call us out if it doesn't look like we're doing enough) and keep us accountable for our goal of a full pipeline of work.

The meeting ends with a roundtable forum for anyone, once again, to say anything they would like to their community, while we're all assembled. This includes public service announcements about taking out the trash and cleaning the toilets as necessary (thanks Momma Tina), birthday and employment anniversaries (thanks James), solicitations for Girl Scout cookies and happy hours, and, for a way-too-long stint, 'This Day in History' announcements from our beloved Dave 'Kern' – no matter how boring this day has historically been. We conclude the roundtable with a drawing for a prize – one person a week gets a chance to spin a prize wheel, with exciting prizes ranging from raffle tickets for ambiguous future prizes, to re-gifted Longhorn Steakhouse gift cards, to $100 cash prizes.

Of all of the components that go into making DBDG such a great place to work, this meeting is, by far, my favorite. I can't speak for everyone, I know (although I'm the only one writing a book about it, that I know of). It's essential in maintaining the level playing field that we, for the most part, try to maintain in the office. It keeps us in lighter spirits, fuels us with inside jokes to sustain us until the next session, and lets us preserve the feeling of community we strive to maintain. Of course, for the less touchy-feely of us, it is also an educational break to get up to speed on how we as a company are doing and what we need to do next. And for the one or two employees who may not care about ANY of that, it's a paid break from the occasional monotony of AutoCAD-ing, emailing, or client phone calling all day to let us catch our breath and refocus for the week-end push. If you're still not sold on its value, I continue to posit that you really have to be there to get it...and if you're ever in the Oldsmar area, we'd love to invite you to join our community for the day and see for yourself. If you can find a way to capture it better than I have, I'll even let you spin the prize wheel – but you'd better land on those elusive raffle tickets.

I Call BS!

Are you not buying that all of our employees love this as much as I do?

You're probably right. We have some employees who go through spurts where they miss more frequently than we'd like them to. And it gets a little implausible that it's that hard to find 45 extra minutes in their schedule that often. The prize wheel was an addition to try and incentivize perfect attendance a little more. But, since we allow our employees to self-manage, we empower them to make the decision whether to attend, and to determine how valuable the information and experience shared every week is to them. Missing is definitely noticed, and we really do *miss* the employees who opt out (whether it be because they really do have to or because of poor prioritizing habits), but we recognize that there is little value in begging people to attend who don't *want* to, and instead focus our energy on the 80+% who regularly attend and make the meeting constantly out-do itself as the best TFM yet.

Do you doubt that everyone cares about our financial standings?

Right again. I suspect that there are several members of our team who totally tune this segment out – if financial analysis is way outside of their UAs, then there's no way they would ever get a lot out of it. I'm also confident that there are a few people who don't understand what we're discussing, or why the numbers change the way they do, or how they work together. To solve these issues, we consistently re-evaluate the way in which we present this information, and try to simplify it as much as possible to keep it accessible without diluting its value. Additionally, like Zoolander's nemesis-turned-ally Hansel, they might not listen to the music that we're making, but the fact that we're making it – they respect that.

Chapter Six: I Shot the Sherriff (No HR HeRe)

We generally like to think that we make the rules, and that we can alter them any time, so that we end up winning. (This is very similar to the way my husband Patrick plays Scattergories©. Whenever he can't come up with a suitable response to the question under the round's assigned letter, he just makes something up, then yells loudly enough until we agree to side with him, lest the police come to break up the game.)[27]

There is one rule, though, to which we hold steadfast and refuse to change: that we are a zero Human Resources solutions company.

Don't get me wrong. We still allow all of our *humans* access to all basic necessary *resources* – we work in high-quality shelter, we are highly encouraged to wear clothing, and we treat ourselves to food & beverage under any excuse. (Oh, Ryan's wife posted another picture of the baby on Facebook?! Unbelievable! Let's get DQ blizzards and then go to happy hour!) But outside of that, most 'traditional' human resources provisions and solutions are hard to find in our office.

---

[27] Examples: 1) Things in the sky beginning with the letter 'G' – God's friends. 2) Dairy products beginning with 'B' – Briérre cheese (when brie and gruyere combine?) 3) Nicknames beginning with 'B' – Bug. I argued against #3, adamant that it is not a real nickname; to earn the point, he called me 'Bug' or 'Buggy' for about 5 months.

Do we have problems? Sometimes, we do. Half of our staff are walking HR-nightmares[28], by traditional corporate standards. The dialogue in our production pit tones it down to a PG-13 rating in respect for Sundays (also, we don't roll on Shabbos.[29]) But we buffer against HR obstacles on the front end, and embrace them on the back. We make a best effort to hire 'right-fit' employees; one of the huge benefits of working in our office is the relaxed, fun, and off-color atmosphere we work in. When you have to work all-nighters – and sometimes, you do – things are bound to get a little weird. We don't want to bring in people who won't be comfortable in that environment, so we try to give them a good understanding, before we even finish a preliminary interview, as to what they're considering getting into.

---

[28] I'm pretty sure the women are the biggest offenders here. If you're ever in the area, ask Cari if you can borrow her coffee cup and check out its artistic interpretation of Stonehenge. But don't ask her who draws the pictures, please.

[29] If you've never seen *The Big Lebowski*, most of this book will be nonsense to you. Please put this book down and rectify immediately.

A Sort-of-Realistic Example of How No HR Affects Our Workplace[30]

---

[30] The following story is fictional and does not depict any actual person or event.

60

So, the above situation might look like an example of sexual harassment, or chauvinism, or one of those workplace no-nos. And, very seriously, I in no way mean to detract from or belittle *serious* offenses of this nature. (I myself was pretty appallingly victimized by this kind of behavior, while working in education a few years ago – it isn't funny and it's never ok.) What I'm trying to highlight here is a level of comfort that exists between co-workers. On the superficial level, it's fun for a lot of our employees to be able to joke with each other without fear that they'll be fired or otherwise severely disciplined. But more importantly, Jan, in this scenario, would have been equally ok in telling them they were out of line, if she took any offense, and these two would have immediately apologized and NEVER spoken to her in that manner again. But rather than having to involve a third party, she is able to make a decision that correlates with her comfort level, and move on. Lucky for crazy Greg and Paul above, this played out in the best-case scenario, and ended with everyone laughing hysterically. Also, we don't employ a bunch of creeps. This would *never* happen in a group of people where this comfort level wasn't already clearly established, and is much more likely in the wake of some carryover happy hour joke.

When situations *do* escalate – and sometimes, they do – we try to learn from them, instead of documenting them in some HR template and putting them in an adult version of a high school permanent record. We encourage the involved parties – often, with an unbiased mediator – to complete a form we abuse left and right from our friends at Strategic Coach – the Experience Transformer™. This document (coupled with the comfort of the culture we've built under the Transparent Organization) allows our employees to talk candidly about specific incidents, review the good and the bad that led up to them, and identify improvement steps for the future. In the last year, we've even shifted disciplinary forms to follow this model – we want to learn from any experience, good or bad – and we want the conversation to be as productive as possible for the affected persons. Generally, during these sessions, we are able to connect a lot of dots as to where communication broke down, and identify simple steps that we could have taken to prevent or minimize stress or angst.

Does this sound like HR? In some ways, it is a little. But instead of going in the employees' files, the relevant paperwork is given to the employees for their review, reflection, and action. The mediator is there to help mitigate any natural human overreactions and refocus dialogue – not to stifle conversation or police tone and diction. Participants are still free to say what they want to say – the exercise would be futile if this were not the case. And, unless specifically designated as an appropriate step in the subsequent actions, there is no 30, 60, or 90 – day follow up session. The file is closed at the end of the ET meeting.

Whenever possible, though, we cut out the 'bad' HR. The Big Brother. The infrastructure that makes no room for life, for mistakes, for transgressions…for being HUMAN. My good friend Jon recently left a firm (which paid him a handsome salary, registering just under six pre-tax figures) because minor disagreements and misunderstandings between him and his supervisor were continuously funneled through the company's Human Resource office, instead of directly with Jon.

One day in particular, he went home during his 45-minute lunch, and was delayed an additional 15 minutes when he found his Labrador had torn his kitchen to shreds and left a series of doggy landmines on the rented carpet flooring. His decision to invest a few minutes into tending to this inevitable and uncontrollable act resulted in a formal write-up, where the HR office let Jon know that he had frustrated his boss. This game of telephone is inefficient and cowardly. The stories are bound to get distorted at least a little through interpretation and re-telling, and more importantly, the element of trust never stands a chance to be developed.

Of course, we have *some* Human Resource needs. We offer our employees health insurance (thanks, Melissa!), and do the legwork to make it a reality every year. We pay all of our people every two weeks (most with overtime as applicable,) so we have to perform payroll services. We comply with OSHA requirements. Supervisors aren't allowed to get physical (Ike Turner style, anyway; time will tell on Olivia Newton-John style) with their team members. We have strict safeguards to protect those unalienable truths. In fact, we have a whole Team Operating Agreement and Employee Handbook to protect against HR minutia. But each of those exists in very basic, low-tech platforms, which I interpret as a testament to the 'importance' we invest in them. Not that we don't think that they are valuable; just, we place more value in one another's abilities to deal with situations as they arise, and to generally police themselves (and maybe their closest friends) to do the right thing. We don't need to pay some executive or third party to tell people what to do, how to do it, and when – each of us is already being paid to make those decisions, under the concept of the self-managing company. And we're giving the knowledge and power under the Transparent Organization and its provisions.

Our Team Operating Agreement, in Summation:

Team Operating Agreement Rules

1. Please don't murder anyone - coworkers or otherwise.

2. Drugs are bad, mmkay?

3. Do what you say you're going to do.

4. We prefer if you not steal from us.

5. If you're going to have a second job, we prefer it not be for our competition.

6. Try not to covet your cube-neighbor's wife.

7. Please don't worship another design or drafting firm as your idol.

8. Don't mess with someone who is hAngry (so hungry they've become angry).

9. Pam does not want to wash your dishes for you.

10. DON'T FORGET YOUR TRASH DAY!

And like I said, we *make* the rules, so we set ourselves up to win from the get-go. If someone's kid has an outbreak of head lice, we offer the flexibility to work from home – and beg that person not to come back to work until the lice are gone and/or all of their hair has fallen out. We've got a couple of delightful germophobes in-house to yell at any malady-riddled coworkers who try to suck it up and come into the office. If an employee has a morning dental appointment because his crown fell out, again, we offer flex time – come in when you need to…just don't make it a habit to be unreliable. Need to take an unexpected leave of absence from work, but not looking forward to a zero-dollar paycheck? Paid Time Off can accrue quickly under our compensation model, and we are pretty generous on allowing employees to sit at negative balances in PTO, on a case-by-case basis.

Seriously, Don't Come in If You're Not Well.

I don't mean any disrespect to Human Resource representatives – as I'm sure I've upset the thousands of current and prospective HR employees who have been glued to this text until now. Many companies have a current *need* for this role. They *need* someone to prevent, solve, and monitor problems. They *need* someone to run to when things don't go their way. They *need* a conduit through which to funnel difficult situations. But what our founder, John Bews, decided long ago (more than two decades), was that he didn't *want* HR. His own years of experience as an employee in traditionally-structured offices soured him on the disrespect, mistreatment, and inefficiency that HR 'solutions' often produce. He was able to connect the dots and identify better ways to handle situations – to make uncomfortable issues much more palatable, and to empower all of us to take ownership of them, so that instead of feeling victimized or belittled by them, we are instead able to grow and improve ourselves and our teammates.

Chapter Seven: Pay For What You Get (Back-Ended Compensation)

There's one more underlying secret to all of the accountability and self-management that I've been holding back from you. It's a huge motivator to work hard, and also a brilliant safety net for your operations during periods of economic downturn. And even though it may be one of the most important cogs in the Transparent Organization machine, I made you wait until the very end to get it. That's not just because I'm a jerk. It's in total accordance with the TO model.

Compensation (monetary and non-monetary) are structured so that a substantial portion is not paid to the employees until the company's annual goal is realized – and then, it is paid very handsomely. This is not to say we are not paid a fair living wage during the year – we assuredly are – but we definitely all look forward to that December package from DBDG Claus to make the holiday season extra happy. The structure of this can get a little complicated, so please see the user-friendly sample chart to help explain.

Davis Bews Design Group Compensation Structure for Permanent Employees			
Item	**Description**	**Unit Breakdown**	**Annual Total**
Hourly Wage	*Your agreed upon base hourly wage; overtime is available to and expected of most positions, and is not included in this figure*	$20.00	$41,600.00
Base Bonus*	*A results-based compensation add-on to be paid at year-end*	10%	$4,160.00
Overtime (based on average of 4 hours/week)	*Your hourly rate when working over 40 hours a week; necessary hours will fluctuate on a client-needs basis*	$30.00	$6,240.00
Quarterly Goal Rewards	*Paid out at the end of quarters 1-3 if quarterly goals are reached*	$500.00	$1,500.00
Total Annual Earnings Potential			**$53,500.00**
Over-the-Goal Profit Sharing*	*Paid at year-end when goal is reached; profits in excess of fiscal goal are shared between employees*	varies	varies
Additional Benefits			
Mental Health Days	Designated 4 day workweeks, available after first full year of employment		
G3* (Company-sponsored vacation) eligibility	Planned and paid company retreat for employee + 1 guest		
QGR (Quarterly Goal Reward) eligibility	Daytime paid event held after each quarter's goal is realized		
*Benefits marked * are payable to employees upon realization of annual D2 billings goal, and payout is based on collections from clients*			
Compensation is generally back-loaded (based on performance and results), so base pay is generally lower on the front-end.			

When a compensation offer is made, it is generally with the "Total Annual Earnings Potential" ($53,500, in this example) in mind, and then reverse-engineered back to an hourly rate. All of the other stepping stones between the hourly rate and the goal are only paid when they happen – if they don't, the employee will still receive *at least* his or her hourly rate for every worked hour, but may not receive all of the other incremental payments.

As you can see, this model clearly incentivizes employees to focus and do whatever it takes to get the job done. The more we all work on helping hit financial billings goals, the more likely we are to reap personal cash and benefit rewards for our work. (And, if you haven't already connected *these* dots, since all of our efficiency metrics are transparent, it also motivates people to hold one another accountable for commitments and expectations.)

The most exciting monetary part of the compensation structure is Over-the-Goal Profit Sharing (OTG). Once we hit our billings goal (and again, progress towards it is published and updated weekly), subsequent billings start to fill the OTG line item. At the end of the fiscal year, this amount is split between all eligible employees (anyone who has worked for DBDG for more than 1 calendar year) as an additional bonus – one not even factored into the original Total Earnings Potential figure. There is no upper limit on OTG – at least, not in theory.

Of course, money isn't the only reward employees seek anymore. Free time is another huge motivator for employees. Our back-end compensation structure affords it to employees in a couple different ways. The simplest: Mental Health Days (MHDs). Every employee has a pre-scheduled 4 day workweek in their calendars, 10 months a year, after being employed for one full year with the company. This means at LEAST one three-day weekend a month is on the horizon (and, since we don't schedule MHDs during holiday weekends, those months come with at least TWO three-day weekends! WOWZA!) This perk is *not* contingent on hitting any client goals, directly – but we still make sure all client needs are accommodated before taking a MHD.

Even more impressive than the MHD provision, however, is the paid week off at the end of December. When we hit the annual billings goal, the office closes from Christmas Day until January 2nd (or whatever the first business day is after New Year's Day, for those of you who want to get all 'technical' on me). This is an entire week of PTO in addition to the time accrued under our own benefits package, and is a HUGE reward for those of us with out-of-town families or children or teenagers at home from school for the break.

Then, of course, there's our Group Goal Getaway (G3). Another reward not presented until we hit the annual goal, but a powerful one. This is a vacation, fully sponsored by the company, for all of its employees and one guest. Among many other destinations, our community has invaded such destinations as Las Vegas, Puerto Rico, and Washington D.C., to appreciate their architecture, indulge in their food and fun, and let Rory sleep on all of their outdoor furniture. It is also a chance for some of us to get to really interact with people we don't get to see very often in our daily routines, so that we can keep that loving feeling going while we make some new memories

Of course, the bummer has the potential to come in, if for whatever reason we do not hit our financial goal. But, there are two important considerations here. First, as I've stated several times – the T.O. allows you to make and manipulate your own rules, and gives you knowledge all along the way as to how to prevent this from happening. Review the budget periodically and start cutting items you know you won't need – we're usually able to cut several thousand unnecessary dollars as we go into November. Cut back on overtime if you don't have the work to justify it (or ramp it up if you need people to put in the hours to get the billings – if you pay it, we will work). Pay attention all along to those metrics and look for anomalies in individuals' performances. Second, if it's one of those years where El Niño wiped out half of your clients' buildable land, and your Enron stock portfolio fell from $90/share to $1/share, and the Best Actor Oscar goes to Nicolas Cage for *Ghost Rider 4: Rider in Space*, at least you and your staff can take solace in this: the decision and sacrifice to be a little more frugal on salary and benefits during the year may not have paid large cash dividends at year-end, but, will have saved the company THOUSANDS of dollars, and will keep employees in jobs for the next year, to start killing it again. This comfort is priceless.

The exact back-end benefits that will work best for your company may be different than these. Maybe you'll have better, more creative ones. Maybe you'll copy ours exactly. Maybe you'll be able to build a buffet of options, so employees have more control over the benefits they want. If you are successful in implementation, though, you can be confident that if you, the entrepreneur, are unexpectedly eaten by a human-created Indominus Rex, or decide you'd rather be riding motorcycles alongside Nick across the Sea of Tranquility, your team will be knowledgeable and motivated enough to hit those goals in your absence.

Chapter Eight: Born to Run (The Conclusion)

I hope you've been able to find one or two ideas throughout this text, or connect a few dots about potential solutions to problems or improvement opportunities in your own offices. Maybe you've even gained some personal clarity about what you definitely DON'T want in your own workspace – we've been down that road a couple of times, too.

As I said in the beginning, the Transparent Organization isn't for everyone – although I wish it were. It takes all kind of communities to build a city, state, country, or commonwealth (or province, for my Canadian friends[31]). Some people prefer a gated community and take comfort and pride in their privacy, and there's nothing *wrong* with that. Hell, we even design some of them in our queue of CAD work. But we prefer an open landscape, where we can watch each other grow, and watch ourselves grow bigger and bigger, too. We prefer freedom from confines of job titles or descriptions, from Human Resources watching our every move and critiquing our every word, and from self-imposed limitation of possibilities.

We've made no secret that our own ideas have been influenced from the teachings of other growth-minded companies and organizations. Dan

---

[31] Shout out to the members of Strategic Coach, our own Matt H., the creators and stars of most *Lifetime* original movies, and a few characters on long-running teen drama *Degrassi*.

Sullivan and Strategic Coach; Joe Polish and the Genius Network; Peter Diamandis and his Abundance teachings, to namedrop a few[32]. That's the beauty of sharing knowledge – we can all constantly contribute to it, manipulate it, change it, grow it, multiply it – indefinitely growing our community of thinkers and doers exponentially.

The steps outlined in this book are only the outline of the changes you'll need to commit to – but if you're interested, you've already been exposed to a wealth of resources, and the Transparent Organization exists to support you in your growth. Reach out to us, via our website, a visit to the Oldsmar area, or tacky stick drawing representing your request. We can't wait to help you change your own rules and connect your own dots on the road to your own bigger future.

---

[32] No direct affiliation with the book – we're just thankful to have had their companies' inspiration on the way.

www.ingramcontent.com/pod-product-compliance
Lightning Source LLC
Chambersburg PA
CBHW060637210326
41520CB00010B/1641